I0180635

Who Do I Have to BE?

DEDICATION

To my favorite and number one person in my life, my daughter Summer Grace without you I would not have come up with so many dreams and reasons to be successful in this life. Giving you all the love I have and all the maternal love you need.

To my mother, you're persistence in showing me the capabilities of a woman continuing to stay on the path of perseverance.

To the women who received advice, mentorship, volunteers of those women who have been a part of my many life stories, your companionship, wisdom, just a simple listening ear has been much appreciated and inspiring. Thank you to those women, elders in my life for stepping in, sharing, and passing along your wisdom.

To my life supporters, new friends, and associates, and those who have yet to cross my path. I send a special thank you.

Love and adore always,
Gracy L. Henderson

For book orders other than individual

consumers, SUM grants a discount on the

purchase of 10 or more copies of single

titled for special markets or premium use.

Mail or email in request. For more

information on how to purchase a book

please see contact information below:

SUM

PO BOX 632322

Irving TX, 75063

SUM_productions@yahoo.com

Who Do I Have to BE?

Who do I have to be?

If I am not your QUEEN?

By

Gracy Henderson

Who Do I Have to BE?

TABLE OF CONTENTS

Who Do I Have to BE?

Chapter 1

Introduction

I wanted to try to invite new ideas or a way of thinking from a woman's prospective on certain topics and situations. I am sure there are many books and a plethora of self-help books to get a person started in the right direction of healthy thinking and assertive thinking. My goals are to give you another example on how to take on situations you may or may not usually address or too embarrassed to admit. Ultimately, it's your choice and your human right as a man or woman to apply the knowledge given or trash it. I would like to

Who Do I Have to BE?

take the opportunity to encourage you to "want" to allow yourself another option or another way of thinking. Perhaps help individuals such as yourself over a hurdle or help with the ideal of understanding self-worth.

The General Population

In general, can mean different things depending upon the context in which is used. When we refer to the general population we look at it from the eyes of what is most popular or what is the norm, in a general sense. There is no limited use of the term but it can be loosely used out of context. Some of the common woes of life are those statuses what we call the "life bucket list". This list starts out with your parent's direction but it ends up with each individual completing it. For example when you are born your parents start the checklist for you. It may consist of encouraging you to have social skills, setting high expectations for yourself in school, staying out of trouble, and staying grounded. Then as you grow from a kid, tween, teenager, into a young adult to finally adulthood hopefully this list has many successful checkmarks to allow you to have a well-rounded fulfillment in life. As you begin taking over this "life's checklist" and on this list it may have; graduate high school, graduate college, select a career, marriage, house, and starting a family on it. Some of those life changing moments in our life cycle are what keeps us motivated at times. There are no easy paths to get there and no manuals on how to navigate. Some of the aspirations are interfered with broken homes, financial destruction, and broken hearts. Let's say this; if you had a manual to guide you through some of the bigger events in your life would you follow it or even attempt to use it? For most of us this answer would be "no". Reason behind this is because each of us has our own imprint and uniqueness. This does not take aware from inquiring or receiving advice on how to evade or get out of a circumstance related to life which is what makes each of so unique. Kind of like your mother telling you what to do when you are young but you refuse, but then by the time you realize it's too late to do as mother said so many years ago. We have to think of some self-help knowledge as the same. We might not need it now but eventually it will cross our path directly or indirectly. Guides to being in friendships, in relationships, new parenting, and new money matters can perhaps help but all of us are uniquely designed to create and do whatever the mind desires.

The issues of life and love, life and relationships, are two of the highest ranking concerns of the general population today, other than divorces and finances being number one. If the general population is on common ground about concerns of new love, great relationships, great friendships, happiness within, great marriages, and successful lives within those experiences, then why not as a population wouldn't we work at feeling and desiring to create those successes? The general populations of men, all feel the same about the concerns of women and the general populations of women, all have the same concerns about men. So if we have been taught $2 + 2 = 4$.

Then we can be taught to correct the thinking and the behavior we allow in our lives.

Power is Limitless

The power of women has not set in so we do not realize it is limitless. We do not understand and I think some of us will master it by the time we hit our 40's but a large percentage of us will not. As women we do not share thoughts, concerns, ideas, and resolutions to issues as our grandmother's did when they were kids and when the elders still raised the grandchildren in the family. We live in a world that has us more disconnected with each other as women than ever. For example cycle consistency; it is a consistent theory. For example, we cannot compliment each other or say anything nice without a condescending agenda to the other person. We cannot meet women without placing a perception on them and with this thought process in place who would want to be in a relationship with you. Think about it, men meet each other and then filter that person into the position in their life they best fit. Women we do not even give ourselves a chance or other women a chance to present themselves in manner to even try to fit into our lives. We are too busy snarling, fighting, and keeping evil intent towards each other in different aspects so much it has become the norm. You have to think how important it was for women to get together and congregate amongst each other in the early years. We have come so far we cannot pay attention to the regression direction in which we are heading. This is how you test yourself. Ask yourself are my only friends the ones I grew up around or knew in high school or college? Have I made any new women friends in the last two years outside of this group of immediate friends? Am I social within new women groups? Now factor in this equation, these groups cannot consist of these following categories:

Who Do I Have to BE?

Divorce party, break up party, exhaling party, misery, sobbing or pity party, or bash him/her party. It's so funny how we tend to support each other when destruction, drama, or anger is the anthem. Women, you must begin learning the value of you. If all women knew their value then regardless of what ratio of men to woman is, most people would be in monogamous and meaningful relationships or marriages. We have to understand no matter where you are at in life men and women are in abundance. You will always have the opportunity to date, relate, socialize, and congregate with the opposite sex no matter what; if social media does not destroy this theory of course.

Even Spike Lee has used his artistic take in his movies to tell you how powerful your virtue is. For example, his movie called "She's got to have it". The general population, the naive woman, just read this and said she was a whore or this movie wasn't good it was just all about sex. Spike interpretation was trying to allow you to see, Nola, was carefree and had a liberal attitude towards sex. The goal was to enlighten you, that a woman can be just as sexual and not belong to a man. Now the flip side of this is the men are chasing her, the men want the relationship with her. Spike Lee did not depict her as a woman. The movie was trying to define the power of a woman being a sexual being and liberated enough to choose the right partner. Now I know you are thinking but hell that was in the 1986 when men back then did not have all the advantages they have now. When women did not have access to enhancements and the degrading factor of women was taboo. True. Well okay let's look at the present. Spike Lee with co-writer Kevin Willmott also did a movie called Chi-Raq in 2015. Its two tells in this story, not only is he showing the war zone of on Chicago's leading crime rate cities. He is teaching women once again the power they possess. He is giving women another perplex, understanding of the power she holds. Now do not look at the fact the

movie was a musical of rap and stereotyped

throughout, that was for the sake of his field

of production to satisfy the people who be.

Break down that naïve thinking then you can

see beyond his political battle of film and

see what he once again was trying to teach.

If you think about it, if women in the United

States alone did this; exactly what the movie

represented, could it or would it truly come

to fruition? Guess what, we can do this but

without even going to the extreme methods

as these movies demonstrate. What I am just

trying to demonstrate, you have men giving

you advice in books and movies from a

Who Do I Have to BE?

liberal approach and your still not listening. Notice another thing Spike does in most of his movies. He uses African American women or natural black women. These women are not only dark in skin color but they have natural features, hair, and natural body shapes. It's sad that only one African American man defines color women as they are in movies, he does not use the prettiest chic or the finest; he uses an example of what a woman of color represents. I can say the same for white or Caucasian movie producers most of them find the average black actor or actress to play lead roles in their movies. They get it even if we believe they are doing it for the other reasons.

Generally speaking black men tend to be influenced by more of the entertainment aspects of living life. So guess what these are the ones who see other races of woman at a higher pedestal than black woman, colored women, African American women, women of color, or urban woman. No matter what your idea or word choice of a black woman is, they come in all shades. As the character Austin Powell would say "we have to get our mojo back".

Chapter 2

Starting the change

Questions help women break down that barrier of self. Really let that sink in. These questions should not only be directed to others, but to yourself. Society tells you, that I, that we are a part of the problem. Guess what if you want change then be a part of the solution.

What is noticeable is every time a woman does something she has to tag the word relationship. Rather if it is a book, movie, speech, or just in conversations. And this is what I mean by this, the reason why men do not take us serious is because we always are seeking a relationship or we always using relationship in our titles to song, books, and script the list goes on and on. It's like blah, blah, blah... to them. You cannot force feed a person who is already full unless you are trying to kill them by gluttony. Let that sink in. I was meditating on law of attraction this week and I said to myself "why isn't there more successful women teaching law of attractions". You have your Les Brown, Zig Ziglar's and your Earl Nightingale want-to-be's representing the males out there but where are the women. I began doing research and I've notice when those women who desire to try to teach the methods of law of attractions they would always use relationship examples as the means of the theory. No, no women we have to stop. We cannot continue to be drill sergeants and press a man or think if we are saying the right thing in the circumstance of a relationship it will happen and they will get it. It is problematic to force feed anyone. It's like a bully telling you to be at the playground after school at 3:00 PM to get beat up. If you were a smart kid you would not show up or think of a clever way in creating a different circumstance. No man or woman wants to be bullied into a relationship with you. I come to realize we as women need some understanding of the word itself first. Yes this word RELATIONSHIP, truly embrace this, you must understand this word is "relationship" tagged in anything is the first thing to send men running for the hills or women to sobbing heart break city. It's not that he does not get it, it's that we ask for something we have no understanding of ourselves.

We are now in a new age and surrounded by technology which puts all women in a whole new league of unadulterated census. Culturally white women have been raised to feel they are superior and they alone amongst all the ethnicities should be privy to monogamous relationships, with the white picket fence, the husband which supports her financially, and their darling kids. White women do not be offended; you were raised with this thinking because it was right and of your own traditional values. Asian, Latino, and Indian women have embedded cultures that determine their husband at a young age and these husbands must present support to the families before a marriage can take place. Rather if we think it is morally correct or not but if you notice I said support (the goat they traded, the personal treasures they traded, etc...) and I also said married (this is to one woman or many women). Other races

Who Do I Have to BE?

of women know they are marriage material; it is taught to them by their parents and passed down by generational traditions. And black women, African American women, or women of color you have been taught and breed to believe you are not worthy of "one of life's most valuable held status" to a woman, such as the success of being married. We do not even carry ourselves or look at the society around us and realize we are the worst of the worse in society's eyes publicly. Behind closed doors there are more tales to tell ladies each and every one of us has a story. Example, the status quo statically shows African American men see fit anytime they come into wealth is when they make a decision to settle down. For the most part this is the statistics of the general population of men. In the case of men of color when they began to have the financial successes of life the shopping list of woman is of a different race. Women outside the race of African American women are more worthy of his hand in marriage and the women of color the few naive or bottom feeders continue to allow him to keep them as his side chic. Falsely, telling themselves tales of excuses to justify the mean of what they are doing. No, no don't blame it all on him; our men are caught up in their own cycle of deceit and transition in this life we live. That is another book from a male prospective which needs to be told. I'm not a man but I do have some understanding of how deceitful the image of men and women are portrayed in this sinister world we live in. Women of color have to understand first they are the only race of women who are ridiculed by all races, they are the only race of women who do not know there foundation or true roots. As a woman of any race, women are one of a kind that were placed on this earth and ordained by a power, way above our understanding which gave us the unique ability to reproduce with any creed, ethnicity, and culture. Who populates the world (we understand there is combination of things contributed by men) and does the sinister world respect that concept? LET THAT SOAK IN. If all this is true then why are we failing in these categories of having the monogamous husband who supports us, those darling kids we desire, and the white picket fence surrounding that beautiful house? Women must start with telling themselves "I know my worth and I am worthy". If majority of society is against you and you are still blaming your mother or father for not hugging you and telling you they love you, guess what! You have to rely on first your spiritual truth and then loving yourself. It starts with you, first. If you do not appreciate yourself, love yourself, or take pride in yourself then why would any person? If every woman decided to know in her heart; if every woman understands she is beautiful, brilliant, smart, intelligent, exquisite, and any other positive noun in her own unique way; we would not be at the bottom of the dating game barrel or out the wife-y lane. Let's go even deeper; if every woman followed her own sprit in which GOD, Jehovah, gave us in the image of him when she laid with a man she would know the worth of it. For example, knowing when she gave her last dime or sacrificed her financial integrity to a man and he spent it on something unworthy, it was not worth it.

When she sold her body to other men for

one man to profit off of it and just plain not

have your own mind, it was not worth it.

There are much more other senseless

reasons we do inexcusable things of our own

accord that is not worth it for a man or any

person. If we could recognize and

understand self then all women even women

of color would be married and be the highest

one on the best trophy wife list to have. We

are in a new day and age, it's not like it was

back in the day when your surrounding

dating pool was just the other women in

your high school. This global internet has

increased our odds even more, so the pool is now four bodies of ocean. Many races of woman especially those privilege from favor such as women of color have to be privy to witness their men with the Kardashian's and Lopez's of the world. They have hips, lips, and bottoms like these women who were genetically given a distinct design. Guess who encouraged that? Men of color once thought their women were on the pedestal which was encouraged by divine culture. Even though the best form of flattery is imitation, it came with a cost or rather a lost. Remember back when outside ethnicities shamed women of color by saying "full lips, big hips, and big butts" were appalling. It was said to be these women being on display

by their own men in videos were considered

fat in the eyes of others; in fact it was

degrading, and unattractive. Now every

block, every corner, every neighborhood,

every state or country, have the same type of

assets imitating a woman of color in how

she was uniquely created. Now in the media,

coverage of hips and lips is in. Do not let the

zero sized models fool you; reality and real

world thickness is in. So now what, what

does a woman of color stand for or do now?

Let me help you, elevate the game ladies.

You are the best innovators by nature. You

are the best creators by nature. You are the

"Queens" by right. It's just lost and you have to regain footing and it starts with you.

Understanding the meaning of "Ships"

We must stop all the woe is me act when it comes to relationships. Understand it first. **Relationship.** Let's define, for the older women, the Webster dictionary states relationship means the way in which two or more people or things are connected. For the younger women Google defines relationship as the way in which two or more concepts, objects, or people are connected, or the state of being connected. Ladies, relate to or connect with; this is the first *law* of relating. It's plenty of women no matter what race in which we tend to force a connection *within* *our mind* that attaches us to a person we are attracted to and hurtfully by understanding and knowing he is not attracted to us. To think as we do, we think this is considered a relationship. **Relate** means to connect in some form of commonality between others. **Ship -** we all know this is boat that holds more than one person and on this boat each and every person on the boat has to be on the same accord in order for them to sail or travel where ever they are going. **Relate – ship**. Get it, LET THAT SOAK IN. Most of us try to connect to those we have no common goals with; we have no common background with, and have no common subject matter in just a simple conversation with. And guess what? I have not even reached the sex, intimacy, and loving parts yet. **Partnership** is defined as the state of being partners. **Partner(s) -** one or more people that work together in business, or sexual relations and it goes on to say someone who participates with another person. **Ship** – here is that word again a large craft for traveling a long distance, it has a mas, an anchor, a bow, a galley, and a stern. None of this works without participation of people. **Partner – Ship**. Get it, LET THAT SOAK IN. Most women do not realize there is no participation with a partner when they are not active with you. In

our mind or in our made up stories to our
girlfriends we tell "girl he wanted to be here
but he had to work" but in reality he told
you to go ahead without him, no concerns
for events you invited him too. Even better
"girl my man proposed, look at this ring"
but in reality you either bought the ring
yourself, or force it by dragging him to the
pawn shop or jewelry store still paying for it
with your own finances. All signs that YOU
do not know what a relationship or
partnership means. Make yourself
responsible for you first. The most important
"ships" of all is the word **companionship**.
This is the yacht! Ladies! This word in its

meaning as a whole state it is *a feeling* of fellowship or friendship. Recognize within the meaning you just gained two more "ships" in one word, look at these two extra ships within the meaning alone as the life boats of this yacht. Feeling like or feeling the support is important to any human being. It is one thing in everyone's life that is requirement of the soul. **Companion** has two meanings: a person with whom one spends a lot of time or one of *pair* of things intended to *complement* or *match each other.* Yes there it is, the Yin and Yang, the equally yokes out there for you Christians. The match for some women may be from the hour, the minute, and down to the last second of everything she stands for and

believes. Or he may complement your ways

of living. Ladies you have to accept men

that match you or complement you well,

understand this refers to something that

completes or goes well with you. If

Christians holds 1st Corinthians 11:3 to be

true: head of woman is man, and head of

Christ is God. Why allow head of woman be

a man who shows, demonstrates, or thinks

she is not worthy or not a precious gem to

him. Dig deeper into yourself worth. It is

important to try or attempt to meet men

where you both are on similar paths, notice I

did not say the same path, just similar. Same

is great but similar is also a great start. Embrace a man who wants to assist in fellowshipping with you because he wants to enhance you or work on making it perfect with you. Do not continue to be with a person who is not supporting in you mentally, someone who does not allow you to have a voice in their life as well as them in yours, someone who is not supporting your own thoughts and ideas, someone who is not supporting your beliefs, and helping with building self-preservations. This does go both ways women. The general population of women overlooks what their own needs are. If you did not need it then your body, mind, and sprit would not need it

to sustain. LET THAT SOAK IN. **SHIP-**
wow! Here's this word again. Keeping in
prospective of companionship, ship in this
term is that yacht. This is not just a boat, it
the *crème de la crème* of boats. This ship
functions just the same as the any other ship
it needs the connection of people to help it
function by participating, it also needs
support to keep it in its immaculate
conditions, and it can be massive enough to
have two supporting life boats. Those two
boats are fellowship and friendship.
Theoretically, I am using the boat analogy to
try to help you understand the terms of these
words to assist in helping you dig deeper

within yourself to make better decision as it relates to these words. **Companion – Ship** this feeling gives you the best of the best. Relationship, partnership, and companionship must all be in line to potentially reach the goal of successfulness of having the capabilities of being in a relationship before ever even thinking about marriage. The best thing a man once told me was "why be with someone who you knew at the beginning does not give you what you need". It was so profound what he was saying we, men and women, are never the one who wants to be the first to end it. Only out of fear. Why wait on drama or why wait until you convince yourself and then all goes wrong then you want to end it. Sometimes;

it should or it can end on a good note before

it ever gets started to head down that world

of drama and that town called sob-vile. So

ask yourself do you want to conquer this

fear to have a better outcome or do you want

to wait to be miserable which can have a

damaging outcome? Why put your beliefs,

desires, vision, or your own voice on the

back burner or at the bottom of anyone's list

or worse at the bottom of your own list. As

women we get into the dealings of trying to

connect to our partners selfishly. We tell

ourselves he will learn to support me, he

will learn my ways, or he will change for

me. WAKE UP. No human being will change for another human being. The mental state of changing is the decision in **ones' own deciding factor of choice** to change. READ THIS AGAIN…LET THAT SOAK IN. We do not have a magic stick to make him finally realize you are the one. Have you ever thought about why every time you meet a man, begin to date, and you immediately tell yourself this is the one. Think about it, EVERY TIME. Ha, ha, laugh at yourself; understand as a human being every time you encounter a new soul to connect with on this earth it is your opportunity to get to know yourself and to apply the good with each step moving forward. EVERY man is not the man for you. People are placed in each other's life for many different reasons but the common theory is for learning to socialize. Ladies we hear all types of philosophers, scholars, and motivational speakers say all the time "do not let anything into your head space you do not want to get in". This should be the same from the top of your head to the tip of your toes. Why allow some of the excuses you tell yourself about men be the reason you head down to sobbing heart break city. You are your worst enemy when it comes to anything in life this includes finances, early pregnancies, careless sex-escapades with men while in what with think in your head what is a so called relationship. You must have a person who connects with you, willing to participate in the connection, and who wants to fellowship with you for the prosperity of both of your lives.

In this new day and age we have very strong go-getter women. This new imperial thinking, we can do what men do. If you agreed with this it is NOT TRUE. Ladies I could never work like a man do not think like a man do not act like a man, nor have no emotional dis-attachments like a man. If your creator wanted this then guess what he would have stopped when he finished creating men. We are valuable, yes and we are so emotional and yes we are

nurtures by nature, and we have the intuition

GOD gave us. You have to know self, have

respect for self, and have this same respect

for other women as well in order to help

break this cycle of behavior geared towards

women. Notice I stated help break the cycle.

Even if you do not see the resolution of

these baby steps in this generation of

millennials, be sure to teach your little ladies

and son what you can and eventually it will

take hold. Everything evolves and is ever so

moving toward change but it has to start

somewhere first. Men say they do not like

the emotional side of women but guess what

it is essential to their needs and existence. If he thinks it does not then tell him to tell his mother he never needed the "let me kiss the boo, boo" when he fell off his bike. Tell him to tell his mom he never needed the "huge" followed by "I am proud of you" when he accomplished something exceeding well in his life. Tell him to simply tell his momma "I never needed one huge, one kiss, no milk, no diapers, or any meals all on that low-income budget she had or did not have". I bet each of these types of mother's will slap the mess out of him. Our nurturing feeds our children. And where did men come from the wound by way of a woman's vaginal canal, a little more complex than that but you get the point. Men do have the nerves and women have the nerve to not only allow it but be disrespectful of their own self-worth as well. Place blame on yourself because guess what we let them. We let society dictate us, but we rank 5 to 3 in most states, we let them dictate images but we rank 8 out of 10 in corporate America. We allow any and everything to happen in our lives be dictated. Get this myth out your head when men tell us were too emotional; release this out of your head. It is in our DNA we do all this by design and by default. Our creator made us this way without mistakes and every one of us is our own masterpiece.

Who Do I Have to BE?

These are core essentials of a woman for which is bound by the law of nature to share with others.

Who Do I Have to BE?

Chapter 3

The Routine

In this day and in this time we have to take back our stance in the status of how we seek a relationship, how we seek partnership, and how to understand when to say no, stop, this is not the person for me. Let's look at the odds. The odds of women to men is not what we been telling ourselves it is. This is just another excuse to feed ourselves to give us a-right-of passage to say it's okay for you to knowingly date a married man, knowingly lay down with a man who has a woman, knowingly sleep with your best friends man, or whatever the dumb excuse is to make your wrong, right.

It is 8 women to every 10 men in the United States now these odds change based on what we see in our states, communities, or surrounding neighborhoods. We start telling ourselves "girl it's no men out there, its 10 women to 1" who told you these odds! Use more than google do your own research; dig deeper, stop passing information either pasted on to you by a bitter woman or a horny man; stop putting myths in the air or circulating rumors. The rumors are making it harder on our younger ladies growing up and our little girls. The reason there seems to be no more men in your area because you have not gone outside your high schools arena, college arena, or neighborhood arena. This is a good one too I am about to tell you about every woman's routine at least between the ages of 35 and above who are single. You get up; you brush your teeth, comb your hair, get a workout in, shower, and pick out the outfit that makes you feel confident for that day only. If you like me you may say your prayers and affirmation as you convince yourself what an awesome day you are going to have. Fix yourself a smoothie, juice, or breakfast before you get in your car to yell at traffic, get to work put in 30% to 45% actual work in, clock out get back in the car to yell at traffic, on your way home you either grab yourself a T.V. dinner or back home you may cook. If you have kids, help with homework, then take a bath, tie your hair down for bed. You may catch a movie or a stupid broken down ex-wife reality show, in reality who never been a wife, to make you feel even less than woman because of the worthless media they are feeding every woman on television. Ladies, then you close your day out by heading to bed with that mess you just saw on T.V. on your mental state of mind. Then most likely you will need to pray again before lying down. This pray is always different from that morning pray. This time you include a few more details such as asking for a man, and then you close your eyes. Hopeless, that is the routine of a woman who is probably screaming "Ain't no men out here for me." If you work in the white collared world as an example, for black women we know the office does not harbor black straight men. And if it does, all the black women in the office are like leeches, they are trying to get with this slim choice of one man but in the wrong way of course. And he is in dog heaven. Now working in the blue collar world as an example black women have plenty of men to choose from but he is usually the guy who is so beat down within his own cycle of poverty or content status he is not the right

man for any woman. He has all those dis-
connected emotional detachments and no
connection with you at all. So women will
do the stupidest things and make a choice to
jump in. Either you are in the pool of
leeches or you fall in that pool of
desperation to settle for the dis-connected
emotional stressor. Both choices disrespect a
woman's own morals and value. Or you
could be the one who does not pick either
and just finish out your daily routine by
what I called, the "go to work and go home"
syndrome. Some excuses are not always the
fault of men out there. You tell yourself it's
too late, too many players out there, or too

tired to go out. You have to put yourself in position to be chased, ladies. Now did I say you have to go to a club or church, **No!** But you do have to get out an about. Doing the same ole routine on a daily can only kill your sprit as a woman. women need stimulations around them to keep them feeling like a woman, rather if this is stimulation from another woman hating on you because you looking so damn good, to a construction work whistling as you walk by going to the store, or an old man telling you "I wish I would have met you in my younger years". Women need the stimulation. Get it, LET THAT SOAK IN. How do you expect to meet or better yourself esteem as a person

if you do not know how to interact or if you
continuously do the same thing day in and
day out. I hear this all the time, you cannot
find a man or put yourself in position to be
chased or to be courted by a man if you do
not break the routine of your same ole
habits. It does not have to be a drastic
changed. Start out light by getting out and
about once a month, then twice a month, but
do not exceed eight times a month.
Exceeding, could lead to desperation. If you
have to go out all the time you're seeking
something you will never find. YOU are
seeking. Get it, LET THAT SOAK IN. Then
you may find yourself in the same ole place

every week or every month. Now what you have done is turned an ole home routine into your outside ole routine. No, no ladies. This type of desperation can also leave you open to anything that comes your way. It will "put out" your internal radar for signs, alerts, and alarms for those men you will need to say no, stop, you're not the person for me. As Les Brown says "insanity is doing the same thing the same way every day".

Who Do I Have to BE?

Chapter 4

Learn how to say "No, STOP, you're not the person for me"

Let's go back to word usage of relationship and partnership. We all want these two words in our lives. How do we go about gaining a healthy, productive relationship that should result into companionship? Understanding both relationship and partnership and know it must lead to companionship. **Companion** in the sense of relationship means one of pair (two) of things intended to compliment or match each other. **SHIP** – THERE GOES THAT WORD again. Ship a vessel for transporting people by sea but this is the yacht.

Companionship is a feeling of friendship.
Most women do not take the time out to be
friends first. How is it if you meet another
person for the first time and you do not
allow some time to go by to build
conversation with him or her, find out if you
both have something in common, and
determine if he or she is trustworthy before
you calling them a friend? Why wouldn't we
do the same thing if it is a man we are
meeting for the first in the scenario of dating
or potential mate? You know why because
we let those good looks, big manly prints
and manly shoulders give us the "tingle and
twinkle". Then we throw all the rational

thinking out the door and before long you're lying down and letting him jump all in your vagina savagely, never to realize you just slept with a stranger. Get it, LET THAT SINK IN, PLEASE. Oh! Now in this particular instance you are not feeling violated because the choice is to be absent of important mental information. To make matters worse we start trying to make ourselves believe just because we slept with this man he is automatically for us or we try to coerce ourselves to ignore the obvious signs to say no, stop, you are not the person for me. Keeping your virginity and finding the same in a partner is always best but in most cases this opportunity has passed.

Women have to realize it is okay to have a "my bad moment, one night stand, or a mistake in choice". It is when you continue to allude yourself to thinking this is okay, he is okay, and he's all I want when you know he does not have the desire nor the attitude of meeting your needs as a woman. Know what it means first: *relationship is the connection, partnership is the participation of both parties in the relationship, and companionship is the combination of these connections which leads to fellowship and friendship of both parties which is one of the essential needs of a forever relationship.* Change you, change your mindset, and understand the endearment of these words first. The faster you get this understanding the faster you will not fall for anything a man or woman throws at you. These words will help you recognize quickly and respond quickly to just say no, stop, you're not the person for me. Secondly, understanding women, what we have to come to grips with is the knowledge men gives us at the start. It's like being a lawyer in court, every lawyer before beginning a trial they will give an opening statement. View this analogy as the same when meeting men. Any criminal will repeatedly do a crime over and over especially if the offender gets away with it. The criminal's job is to design the perfect and simplest solution by taking the less exposed path of risk to commit a criminal act without getting caught to satisfy a need. This need can be personal, psychological, or for financial gain. If this criminal is never caught they will continue to repeat what works. Again, view this same analogy with dating. Women when meeting men notice he will always have an opening statement. If he has been living long enough in the real world he has a compelling opening statements which will work on just about every genre of women. Every woman has their own certain level of what they will allow and not allow from an opening statement. This means what you will allow by looking over it and what is considered zero tolerance, this are things you will not allow or not let slide by. All women should have thresholds. Now this does not mean to have a stupid, naive, or unrealistic threshold. For example "I do not want a man with kids" this puts you in a bind if you have children yourself or if you do not have any children". You've just put yourself in lower level pool of men selection. All men do not have "baby momma drama", all men are not bad fathers and all men should not be stereotyped by thinking they are not taking care of their children, and all men are not dogs. Stop spreading these myths and rumors. Come to understand this; the most obvious and desirable men are not always the obvious choice. Now I am not saying go get an ugly guy either. I am stating good men are hard to find not because we assume they are not out there but because it requires us to take a little closer look at attributes before discovering him. Women have lowered their standard at some point in time. When we are looking at TV, videos, and movies we see everyday men haven't lowered their standards. Bigger lips, breast, and booty are throughout the media, in fashion even in cartoons. Who run this world? They are men, so if their standards have not changed then why should ours change. They want a woman with tight skin, nice hips, and a tight behinds rather if she is slim or not. Intelligence, wisdom, and educated along with this is only for those select few of men out there. We do whatever we can do to fit this persona for just the assets only. We need to ask ourselves for the same things and have the same requirements. Homosexual men make sure they look good for each other. We have to ask for the same conditions for heterosexual men, they need to look good for us. You have to tell yourself not to settle over and over. Here you are working out, getting liposuctions,

and squatting for them thunder thighs in the
meanwhile your choice of men do not fit
your physical needs. Do you ever wonder
why we fall for the fine men so quickly, who
we know is dumb or unintelligent? Because
it is the physical that attracts women to him.
When your meeting, greeting, and flirting
with men make sure he is up to your
standards too. Now I am not saying there are
not any fat fine men out there. There are
some men who are more than willing to get
in shape for you or workout with you. Going
back to the basic principles of getting to
know the men you met first. When you get
to a certain age ladies sex, intimacy is not to

be played with. When you're young, you are still getting to know your body and you are still usually playing around partying, having sex with anything with a penis in his pants. As you gain maturity pussy begins to cost. Hate to sound so vulgar, perhaps you do not want to look at it like that but it does. Who does it cost? It is a cost to women, not men. Men do not care about your emotions and feelings behind giving them some vagina. Understand it is just something to satisfy the moment. Men will go through leaps and bounds to have sex with you for the first time. I do mean ANYTHING, it is his goal to conquer your private sector. This is not new information. It is your power and your choice to give that part of yourself up. Pussy cost time spent, pussy cost you emotion, pussy cost you devotion, and pussy can cost your dignity, integrity, car, house, marriage, children, respect, family, and your soul. It does not matter how soon you give it up or how long it takes you to give it up, it is the responsibility behind the decision when you do.

Chapter 5

Who wrote the best book?

Do not believe some of these books men write to tell us how we need to be in order to get them. Look at it as tips but no man knows a woman better than someone who can experience the same thing, wisdom and knowledge of a woman. Ever thought why the books are never written in the other direction; "act like woman, think like a man" yeah hilarious huh but think about it. Men have no wisdom of a woman's travels through life; each of us has a story. Even men have a story to tell us. They do not understand vaginas, cycles, birthing babies, hot flashes, dildos, and how we can work 8 to 10 hour days in the workforce and turn around then do another 6 to 8 hours with our children. Including having inconsiderate men at home added to an already full plate of life and still keep our sanity. A warrior or solider cannot tell what a seamstress needs, the sun cannot tell the moon where it needs to be. Get it, LET THAT SOAK IN. No woman! So come down off that high horse of yours as well. You cannot tell him how to be a man either. Take a deeper look, how can all the books written by men be for women, for example like how women should act for him or to get him? Hell, give women some real advice about self-worth.

Telling women what we need to be in order to be considered in being their woman, can women turn the table? Realize those tips they provide work for that type of person who wrote the book. Realize those tips work for different type of men and for the benefit of these men. Note this: but if a man believes you know the game then why wouldn't he change it up again, and again, and again. The same game used in the 50's by men is surely different in this millennium. As long as there are men like Mr. Harvey giving you the game just believe there is another man out there stepping up his game or changing the game because of the information spilled. So now Mr. Harvey's knowledge you read is 9 years old. Stop following for anything, ladies we must understand when a man tells us to our face, straight up out of his mouth, these things you must take it as a tip from him:

1) I am focus on my career, I am not looking for a relationship.

2) I am not looking for a relationship so we can be cool with this understanding that we are just kicking it or having fun.

3) I am this way and I am not changing.

4) I love all types of women so you have to deal with the player or not.

5) We can kick it time to time but I cannot make you my main girl.

The sad part is you do have women who can resist at first. They are like "well we just can be cool friends then." Then the man is your friend and because he shows you he can be just that "friend" you want him to be. Then at some point you decide to want him to be more than a friend. The trick is if you take the advice of the Harvey's in the world and give yourself some time to evaluate the friendship you would know in a split second what the true intentions are. The problem seems to be we cannot outlast the men on temptation of sexual relations these days, but in some cases we are worse than some of them. You began fishing or reaching beyond his features, his career, or whatever you did to excuse yourself from not paying close attention to his opening statement; he was telling you what it was or how it is going to be. It is your choice to make the wrong decision. Now all of sudden you notice all the attributes you think your missing just because you are not having sex with him and he is playing the role of a friend very well for you. These silly mind games women tell themselves or made up in their own minds are very much a part of the problem women place on themselves.

The cycle is endless. YOU CANNOT CHANGE HIM or WAIT ON HIM TO CHANGE. All these answers above means your easy, you are not my girl, you are someone he just wants to has sexual intercourse with if you allow it, and that is all you will be. RED FLAG, he is not lying to you this is the most realist or honest he can be with you. Why because he gave you your choice. If given the one thing most of the general population is asking for, the choice to choose. We are the new age millennium women. We are always saying

Who Do I Have to BE?

to men just be straight up honest with us or just be truthful. If he would have told you he was already dating someone first it would allow the choice of you deciding if you would rather continue to kick it or moving on. Choices! Then when a man tells us straight up, and gives you your choices, women act like he has not even said a thing to them. Women ignore not only what he has presented to them but the truth of the matters behind the heart, allowing him to have the opportunity to make you pick your face up off the floor when you see him with someone else. When you realize he's never going to be in a relationship with you, when he still conditioning you to only come over

in the "come get it hours", or if he is simply
ignoring you all together after he conquers
his quest. Women have now been
conditioned to all dudes "new game" to give
them their choice but we have forgot why
we requested or wanted this type of choice
in the first place. We asked for this choice to
be able to have a response and the
confidence to answer with an okay, no, stop,
you are not the person for me, or with an
exit greeting of well it was nice meeting
you.

As a woman you have to stop and say to
yourself and them; you are not the person
for me, no, and move on. There are plenty of

men out there who are single and even if they are not the right one at least you do not have to worry about getting caught up into a life full of drama and circumstances. What are these circumstances you say? AIDS, HIV, STD's, and by the way have you watched the documentary show snapped. Women lost their courage when they asked for the freedom of choice, and got it. The "new game" has caught on. We have women that are getting told the truth, then when they get hurt or when it does not turn out the way you planned it, guess what? You just have set yourself up for failure. What you have done is allowed that man you chose to embark on you with this no strings attach escapade to sleep with you. He who has admitted to you he has a wife or a main girl. That man who has clearly stated he is focus on his career first and is not seeking to have a relationship at the moment but he still wants to savagely jump up and down in your vagina. You have secured him with the best ammunition, at the end of the day. So when you get to the point where you think he is going to embrace the fact of being in a relationship with you, the side chic, you think he is going to cave. Or when you think he has spent enough time with you to finally change for you, ha… ha… he hits you with

Who Do I Have to BE?

the best response and you have no choice
but accept it, read as followed:

1) I already told you I had a main girl,
   didn't I?

2) I told you I was not looking for a
   relationship at the beginning, didn't
   I?

3) I told you we can just kick it and you
   chose to agree to just kick it with no
   strings attached, didn't you?

4) I told you not to wait on me didn't I?

5) I told you I was still in love with my
   ex or baby momma at the beginning,
   didn't I?

Now you're suspended in stupid-vile
looking at him with tears all welds up in

your eyes, your heart all in the seat of your pants. These tears are not going to work they are just a temporary fix for him to whoa you again, hit it one more time before he still walks out the door, and then the pain picks up where it was left off. What can you do or say, nothing. Now your like gossip to go with the soap box, calling all your girls who told you in the first place don't do him, crying, drinking wine until you are piss-y drunk, sadly depressed, going through the hate-every-man rampage, in turn you are turning YOUR OWN self into a bitter woman. Now you aren't eating or eating too much, yourself esteem has dropped even lower than before, and you have no self-worth until the next man comes along. No, no ladies. No need for the pity party you did it to yourself and if you had the real women friends around your circle they would continue to give the harsh reality of making you responsible for your action or the choice you made. Oh but remember we do not have those types of friends those were the women we did not give the opportunity to get to know. So we create the pattern of hurt and depression then you start to thinking well when I get me another man it will get better. Oh but remember we still have the cycle mentally thinking EVERY man is the one. So not only have you not healed from your hurt you just carried it into the next potential relationship. "When you move on to the next man", here is the problem with this approach. You have not allowed yourself some re-coop time. You have not had the time to understand your own failure nor understand what made the relationship bad. Women must take these lessons from this failure, the new knowledge that is obtained from putting yourself through this and then apply it in a positive way in the next round. For example, it's just like job skills. Your very first job; you were brand new, no knowledge of how to interact with customers you just did whatever the job required you to do. After being employed there for a while you become accustom to the position. You leave the first job for its cons but there were pros. You are now going into the next job the bad or cons, you know how to look for it and avoid it at all cost because you have learned some lessons from the previous job situations. The good or pro stuff you take along and apply it to the next position in congruent of learning or retaining new knowledge. Which the previous knowledge that is now called experience will help you to either further your career or help you in your future career. And so and so on until you are confident enough and obtain years of experience in your position to now call yourself an expert in your career field or profession. Then at this point you know what you are worth and how much your employer should pay you for your experience. So why wouldn't we as women apply the same concepts to dating and relationships. Take the bad and learn from it but remember you must throw it out first and get over it quickly. Learn from it, be careful not to harbor or hold on to it and carry it into the next relationship. As you travel through life this process will also help you determine what type of man you need to seek you. The bad, the cons, helps you get to the good, the pros. LET THAT SOAK IN. You WILL fail more times in your life span before being successful. It is how you get back up or get back in the race, how you start the process over again but take a different approach. This helps many women be successful not only in their life but in knowing themselves when in a relationship.

Who Do I Have to BE?

Chapter 6

What is the approach of knowing what fits?

I see you now trying to figure out what I mean when I say it helps you as the individual woman you are to figure out what type of man fits your needs. Why do you think you need a man in your life? Why do you want to be in a committed relationship? Are you ready for a relationship? Why do you want to be married? And are you woman enough to have this status? When we are young ladies we allow teen movies on T.V. to embed into our minds what type of dude we think we want. For some of us

who were blessed to have a responsible
father's in the household, you are usually the
women who have the best example of a male
role model. These women tend to want a
man who emulates their father "if he is truly
a loving, providing, supporting father" that
is. For those of us left who have no father
figures in our lives this is most important for
you to understand. When we are young they
program getting married, happily ever after
stories, the dream teen who looks like the
best hunk, and he is with the prettiest girl.
And that pretties girl is always us in our
imagination. We live with this imaginary
image from grade school to elementary, then

Who Do I Have to BE?

middle school or until we get our very first boyfriend and most likely he is dreamy in our eyes to start. We set ourselves in the bubble of TV love and happily ever after's. Then guess what, the reality of relationship begins to set in. The first boyfriend breaks up with us and we act like we in the movie or the soaps, well some of us do, but some of us realize "hey is this how it goes?" Things begins to click, so either they add up or do not. Some of us learn and get better at it and some of us turn into those chicks who carriers the flash lights in the daytime looking and lurking around Tyrone's momma house cause we emotional unstable by the time we are mature enough to understand what relationships are. How do you stop the madness, first understand TV is for entertainment purposes only. Turn it off, live life. Life teaches real world lessons. Especially turn off these reality shows! Think about it if there was no drama in these shows we would not watch them. FYI they are STILL SCRIPTED which makes it not a reality. Most of us who are real women can only stand so much of a misrepresentation of woman on TV we are smart and intelligent enough not to support such a massive teaching of ignorance. But those other foolish girls, ladies, and women do not realize the demise of our women willing to emulate this non-sense they watch on these types of shows. Think about this, we had teen shows when we were little children. Now we have adult shows that show women in the wrong light and if we continue to ingested the foolishness we are damned to all be baby mommas and unhappily married, or ex-wives. Another comparison, why are all the rich reality shows all have husbands with a few exceptions of TV drama. All the mob women reality shows all have husbands and money, and these are high profile criminals who are in jail but not even shown in that light, they are glorified instead. THINK ABOUT THAT ONE, LET THAT SINK IT. Then here we go with all the black

women reality shows were they are all ex-
wives freshly divorced or getting divorce,
some did not even make it to wife status just
ex- girlfriends, not as wealthy as the other
shows, and we see proposal to men who do
not obviously want to marry them. A whole
bunch of dysfunction they feeding women
and crippling the mind of our young ladies.
This is making them think it's cool to be just
the chic on the side, the ex, the side piece,
the complainer, the instigator, or the baby
momma. And we wonder why we do not
have good men because they look for those
women you see on these types of shows.
They are training women. Stop, turn these

Who Do I Have to BE?

shows off! Trust and believe there is always enough drama in our own lives to be entertained on instead of feeding our minds with this consistent negative non-sense of how they think women are portrayed. Once you start to understand we do not need to put our lives into a TV show or movie setting, you will then begin to wake up just a little bit more to awareness of self-worth. Get it, LET THAT SOAK IN. We are in the real world we are human, we are Queens, and we are worthy of the same worth. This is what I mean by getting us back to the status we are meant to be at. This gives women a clear example of what level we are at as women. Men who love drama like this are usually the same ones telling you "I am

not looking for a relationship but we can be

sex friends" and you accept all the drama

that comes along with the circumstances and

choice you made.

Chapter 7

Understanding Signs

Not only men but the things around you, your heart, your intuitions, and sometimes your creator will just flat out tell you if you are in the wrong situation with a man either clearly through a dream or a simple verbal confirmation through just the contact of another person who has value in your life. As you've heard it before many times, but women tend to ignore it, it's called intuition. Every woman has a natural intuition censor specially made for her, but you are not in tune with it. These are usually the women who throw it around verbally all the time when they think it helps to tell the guy about their own sensor. For example, a woman may just see her man getting ready for work, a normal thing right? But because she has not mastered her understanding of her own worth, because of her own misguided thoughts, because she just has not let the bad stuff in the old relationships go, and because she has failed to understand the meaning of relationship, partnership, and companionship her little bitter evil twin in her head tells her: his is cheating. ***This isn't intuition***. That's your - all messed up mind. It's so funny, let me help you understand. Mature women who know their worth stay in tune with their personally designed sensor. If it kicks in as a *woman* of this caliber she will just listen and move on. She will do this without a fight or without needing closure because she knows God put something in her for the purpose of understanding her own sprit. You never hear about this particular subject in advice gear toward women written by men. Men cannot tell you this in their books. They have the same intuitions too; do not let them fool you. As you mature you have to understand some things and situations do not need closure, its simply the best thing for your life, for your sanity, or for your well-being to listen to your own personal sensor.

This information is especially for those women who find themselves in abusive or mentally abusive relationships. The type of behavior of many mentally or physically abused women in this day and age is not because the abuse was passed down generationally to them. It is the carelessness of what we allow. Being a woman means understand your gut feelings about some things; it can save your life when it comes to matters of the heart. Just like a twin knowing when their sibling is in a situation across town, just like mother feeling something is wrong with her child a long distance away, it's the same in the instance of relationship. In most cases we have signs already pointing in the direction we need to go in. Then when intuition kicks in after receiving a whole lot of signs, a whole lot of confirmations, then this means you are about to get hurt in the matters of the heart or your life depends on you listening to your intuition. At times its best to put the brakes on and move on immediately. Women you must begin to listen to your own struggles, listen to your own heart, and know your worth. As I discuss earlier you have to dismiss and

understand the bad but move on and apply
the good going forward.

Chapter 8

Know the difference in being a side chic

It is sad in a sense that women do not even play the role of a side chic correctly. I am not encouraging being the side chic but I do want you to understand some differences when it comes to different back grounds. Haven't you notice any Hassan, African women, Asian, and Italian cultured women do not play the role of a side chic it is rare if they do. If you do not believe me take your own survey. Ask all the women in different cultural backgrounds at your job or in your community function events, how their culture handles these matters surrounding relationships and marriages? You should ask women with deeply rooted cultural backgrounds this question and they will immediate give you a look or think "how stupid of a woman you sound". Let's look at African women when you examine the fact they maybe the 4th or 5th wife of their husband you have to understand the side chic thing is really none existence. Here in the states of course the land of the free things, culture behaviors, and family traditions are thrown out the window when it comes to dating, relations, and marriage some for the better some for the worst.

When the husband decides to court another women to add to his list of wives it is a process of cultural traditions and behavior. So not only is she not the side chic, he does marry her and take her as his wife. You ever asked yourself why? Do your own research.

Some of us live in the states so I cannot constitute it as okay, but it is the culture. The key point is not being a side chic. Some side chic's goals are to become the main chic. Ladies if he has already told you, you are only the side chic then move on if this is not your goal. Say no, stop, you are not the person for me. Some women play the role as side chic well but there are those who play the side chic great with main chic capabilities. Let me explain. If you choose to be the side chic and then make sure you reap main chic benefits. If you want to lower the percentage in being the side chic then we have to step up our game as women. Let's take these two different side chic's as an example, we all know initials KK the family that is making a load of money off of what started out to be on one members assets only and then there is the video vixen who wrote the "tell all book" about sleeping with hip hop, singers, sports celebrities, and many other predominate names. Both ladies have been with many men as the side chic and/or the main chic. But let me point out the differences. KK played the role of a side

chic with main chic benefits but gain the

notoriety from porn. The video vixen played

the role of a side chic but gains nothing.

What was gained was only to be a topic after

the fact and she did not gain the notoriety

from the same role and positioning. KK gain

respect and gain loved, and her porn was

then forgiven by the public and her

reputation soared which put her and her

family at new heights. The vixen has no

respect from the public, will never probably

have the opportunity for love because of the

reputation. But if you notice they both did

all of these things which the public was

witness too. So ask yourself did race play a factor? No, I think not in this case. It's the fact one woman knows how to play side chic with main chic benefits and the other one does not.

If you are currently playing the role of a side chic ask yourself these questions:

- Is he calling you or texting you on his own terms?

- Is he taking you out from time to time? Outside of special occasion's ladies when he cannot?

- Does he call to only entertain the thought of you, even thou you are the side chic?

- As the side chic, is he dictating where you can go, what you can do, or the instructor of your life?

- Is he keeping things interesting for you?

The side chic who only gets called or texted before he comes over to have sex, or the side chic who never goes anywhere who always allows him to come over and has no desire to even pay for a room, and the side chic who allows so much space it turns from being exciting to you to feeling you're doing it just cause you can. The side chic is the woman who has no clue how much power she holds. Ladies this is not me telling you to say or go do something stupid. I am not reigning on the goals of being a one woman man, in a strong relationship. It is a finesse of the things you ask for as the side chic. The reason some woman do it better than you is because they know how to play the role to benefit them. Let's face it we technically do not like the term "used". Hell let's face it, both parties in a situation of being the side chic are being used. He is using you for excitement, attention, and sexual needs so keep in your thought just because you're the side chic does not mean he should not meet your needs as well. We have a bunch of thirsty women out here in the real world. If we just pump the breaks a little and get some of what we need; if we do not want to be the main chic or if you're one of those who are just so content with fooling around with someone who does not belong to you, than let's be for real, do it right.

Now I know you're wondering what I mean when I say with main chic benefits. If you are a side chic your job for him is to give him his space, know your role, never ask questions or never try to have the "talk", and play out all of his desires. Even if this means you're jumping off ceilings and chandeliers landing perfectly. In your role you must be faithfully silent, and deadly in

Who Do I Have to BE?

bed. Now let's reverse that thought. His responsibility to you to keep your silence is to make sure you get not only what you need but what you want. Understand what I am saying this mean, yes you must enter into an agreement to keep your silence. Meaning, explain vital details of what your contract requires and important information to satisfy your needs and wants, to be able to make sure to keep your cooperating silence. The fellows might not want to hear this but hey you already both in a drama-filled situations that could turn into SNAPPPED in just an instant. Side chic role with main chic benefits can be, simple example, assuring he calls, or text you on a schedule to your liking. Now this does not mean everyday but this does set your expectation as the side chic. Make sure you understand you are the "trophy" in this situation. What I mean side chic with benefits get "showed off". He might not take you to events that incorporate special events but note he also needs to entertain you and keep it interesting for you, especially if you're the side chic without a main dude of your own. This means establish arrangements, he will take you out to events. Let me explain something, this means you have to understand this may mean he will take you out of town or across town or only introduce you to certain friends. What this does is allows you to satisfy some emotional needs to compensate for not being the main chic. Basically fellows it is helping her stay at bay when it comes to certain things. Within this required time and schedule calls, finesse anything you need on your end. Ladies not asking you to go "gold-digger" crazy, this means just make sure you are asking the appropriate questions about him to even see if the side penis is even worth it. The finesse allows you to get a better understanding of treatment he is going to give you during this temporary situation. Yes I said temporary. Again I am not telling you to be the side chic only, just giving you better tips on playing this role. There are so many ladies who play this role and in reality you think by being in this position you will get ahead. You have to think of it as if it was your job. Telling yourself "if I stay dedicate and work really hard I will get the promotion" this only works in a career or job situation not as a side piece. This only mentality translates toward sexual relationships. 98% of women who find themselves as a side chic end up not happy, heartbroken, and you're not asking yourself what benefit am I really getting even if I have provided the tips of being the side chic with main chic benefit. The goal here is to discourage you to be that chic. The goal here is to help you understand we have to want more for ourselves. Only a few things come from being a side piece:

1) This woman is okay with being the side chic because she has no life, or she has no self-esteem, or no self-worth.

2) This woman thinks by being his side chic she can take him from his main chic. Turns in to a quest to destroy another woman or family for gratification.

3) This woman will actually benefits in other ways, while playing the part.

4) This is a woman who despise cheating but justifying your situation as the side chic.

Why allow this? A side chic is not the path to go but let's make sure you get what you need and want out of it. Just random sexual contact is not what you need. Without a doubt what goes around comes around in life. Live life positively as you can and the return in rewards will come. Do not be a side chic.

My plea to men

I have to account for both sides when writing this book. I have come to the conclusion not only women need tips about men. Men need tips about women. Biggest question what do you want? Just sexual pleasure and a quite mouth, huh? Let's go back to the famous line to women "I am not looking for the relationship but we can kick it." Own up to this, be respectful and share minimum amounts of time, this includes not meeting or introducing important members into the respect grounds of limitation. Guys, respectfully you cannot make statements such as "you are just kicking it" when your action show more. Actions always mean more than words, some dudes are making the statement of not wanting to be in a relationship but do not define a respectful boundary. This is what I mean: you cannot say to women "I do not want a relationship"

but in the same conversation say "we can

see where this goes." This is an oxymoron.

You are contradicting your state of not being

in a relationship theory. You're saying no,

but you're inviting the ideal of it. It's not

fair to women to continue to keep them in a

constant state of confusing. Another

example is your actions, work on keeping

respectful distances. This means do not hang

with your side piece every day or night,

even every other day is bad too. Do not ask

her to cook or clean for you or do vice versa.

The reason why I say this is because doing it

repeatedly is considered time spent or a

show of interest. When two people or human beings are spending time with each other these are considered valuable moments for not only her but you as well: these moments cannot be erased, returned, or do-overs. Some guys do not look at it that way but this is the process of courting or getting to know one another. If you call a woman, given an unexpected conversation or knowledgeable conversations about yourself and there is an exchange of engaging dialogue between you and her how else should we view it? Please explain how else we are not to look at as start of relationship? I am pleading with men to refrain from defining action of playing grown or playing house, wanting all the perks of a girlfriend or wife behaviors with action and thinking your words are more valuable than your actions. Do your best at spending just enough time, do your best not to meet the parents or kids, do your best to keep personal responsibilities such as cooking, pick up kids, running errands, or cleaning for you at a minimum when requesting. This also means fellows only cook if it is apart the date arrangement. Only in emergency or in dire need circumstances should you ask for other requests such as these. I agree there are some silly woman out here who read between thin lines as well when you are keeping it limited but please understand there are some men who are falsifying there entire hidden agenda. Men you cannot keep placing responsibility on women as if it's always our faults in the misinterpretation. Those men who claim they did truthful tell their women what they wanted. Half of us are high-capping amongst friends but reality is, we really do not truthfully tell each other the blunt truth. Women we will accept the confusing or the contradicting statement and will not challenge a man to be clear with us. If you do not understand a man statements ask questions, keep asking question until you put enough pieces together to understand the underline agenda. Stop giving a shit about him getting upset too when he is answering.

If he does this then stop and move on, red

flag. This is why the questions early on like

other written authors such as Mr. Harvey

suggest. Majority of the time the underline

agenda will always be sex ladies so stop;

please stop acting like that is huge problem.

We tend to all make up our mind in the first

few moments of meeting if he or she is sex

worthy. These issues we have to resolve is

getting a clear understanding of the agenda

which most times always affects the heart,

or the emotion of it all later down the road.

If you want a relationship know the agenda

before you give your prize possession away.

Who Do I Have to BE?

Men tell us all the time, the woman has the control of the entire situation it is his job not to mess it up before he gets the draws. Some of you ladies who have good relationships with your brothers, fathers, or any men in your family need to take the time to ask them some questions. They can give you the game every day but it seems the men are evolving their game better than women. I hate to say game but I meant the chase game of championship.

Fellows, what happened to wanting to be that guy to marry a woman worth marrying? We all have our theories as to what satisfies us and we are all at different levels in life. Why is it the general population of guys marrying stripers, porn stars, and sex vixens just because of banging body or notoriety? I was told a few times by men the reason behind this is because men view these women as hustlers; they know they will go out and get it by any means necessary. Is this true? Do you really want your woman to go get it by any means necessary? When you have sex or intimate relationships are you not thinking about she could be going out there by any means necessary and bringing it back? Whatever it is? There are plenty of women who go and get it by any means necessary which does not require such a demeaning career choice.

Who Do I Have to BE?

There are more women who are business owners and CEO's now than it has ever been. This only tells the general population of women who are in this brackets it's the control that counts and not the money or the hustle. It's not all about control, is it? It cannot all be for the reasons of being not able to control or not dealing with the stress of truly intelligent, successful, smart, humorous, and goal oriented women, is it? I am not going to tell you how to think or going to tell you what is best for the general population of men and I am not going to tell you what type of women you should date because to each its own. All I am asking is what is the problem? For example, what happened to men of color wanting to marry women of color? What seems to have become all too familiar or common result is men of color is when he finally gets his satisfaction in life which is "stability and finances" he then does not want that woman of color but another. Selfishly, you date black women all your life until reach the point of success then you make the women of your race feel they are not even worthy of being married too and marry outside of your culture pool. Men you do know we do have exciting, exotic women from different backgrounds or wealthy backgrounds who are women of color as well. It's not that I

Who Do I Have to BE?

see a problem being married to other cultures or outside your race it's just we see a diminishing the numbers of black love. A white man can be sharing the same plea with white woman. There just seems to be a higher ratio of black men with other races after wealth than black women with other races after wealth. Generally most of these men who are successfully embrace marriage with other races than they would with the relationships they have with their own culture.

This is more of plea to not allow media influences to desensitize your thoughts for those women. We are all living in a world where we take a beating in all different direction and we have to do better as a culture to try and replenish black love and marriages. Those of you who are married have to understand is it not okay to cheat/commit adultery. The effort which is put into to cheating can be put into trying to fix your marriage. And if the marriage is not working then it has to be okay to understand to bring it to a close before involving yourself with someone else on the side. Men there are a whole lot of women all over the world. The point is, men you cannot get with every woman in one life time.

If you are trying to accomplish such a goal then work harder at not having a main chic or even attempting in being in a relationship. Respect yourself and other women enough to tell them your intentions and hidden agendas. Let me explain, some men will say exactly this "I am not looking for a relationship" but your actions can speak louder than words sometimes. Men have women they want to just have sex with but at the same time you are calling, dating, and enjoying each other's company consistently. Instead of saying "you not looking for relationship" just say "at the moment I am not in a relationship". Do not repeat the same woman over and over because eventually she is going to take note of the interest as something else. Ladies it has come to my understanding it allows men not

to speak into existence loneliness. They

have needs as well, they will and eventually

in some cases want this later in life. It is not

okay for a 40-55 year old man to be thinking

he is still a player, thinking he still looks

good enough to get a young lady and make

her marriage material. By changing the

direct approach of what you do not want to

be in or what you do not want to have can

block you from a blessed situation. All

contact with people period allows for

learning. As the saying goes some people

are in your life for reason, a season, or life

time. If you say what does not happen or

what cannot happen then if you do find yourself in a dating scenario where you begin or think you want to build on or end up liking the woman, then if you notice you have already closed that door on the possibility. Men you should not continue to act as if you do not have feelings or emotions. It is more than likely you will not have them at first or display them right off the bat, stop telling yourself what you won't or will not do. Life will sometimes test you and put you in a position to change your whole way of thinking in a moment. Divorced men, you will eventually get off the hating of the ex-wife, it may take you a little longer, but you will. It cannot continue to be used as an excuse for decades after you've been divorced. If you have went through a bad relationship all women thereafter cannot be treated as only sex objects or with the disrespect you did not have the courage to use on that ex. The general population of men I plea with you to learn from your relationships and take on some responsibility in understanding you played a part in making that bad decision when dating or when you married that ex. Vanity is a big issue with men when it comes to choosing the wrong woman. There are signs for you as well when a woman is with you just for your money or possessions.

Who Do I Have to BE?

We have some trifling woman in the world that is just as sinister. If you get with a striper or porn star understand you may be looking at the money flow when you first meet but turning her into a house wife. Come on, you are bond to get some issues out of that.

In this day and age men are not like they use to be. More men were driven to work, be supportive, and one day provide for their families. If you have notice the baby boomers are now older and this is when the rate of single parenting escalated. Now we have a new generation of men who have only been raised by women and on top of this we have so much estrogen in the food we eat now days, it makes more of you act like bitches than the women do. This is probably why some of you guys are confused why you are growing man boobs. There are more men who talk more than woman and they do not mind communication anymore. But the one thing we are losing out on are men who understand support, protecting, and family. These new emotional men, women, may be in tune better on an emotional level, but they are not trying to be the man or the King of the castle. Not working, living with your mother or with your main chic, and not financially taking care of yourself. The sad part is and you want us as women to wait until you get those two things "stability and finances" together. That's a joke because in most cases you're so far behind in reaching or even thinking about these goals. Your waiting until you are in your mid-forties or early fifties before you even make an effort. Think about your life I am sure that one girl friend you had asked, supported, or tried to encourage you to figure it out a way before you hit your forties. Men, even your mother in some cases, have told you to get off your ass or try to lend you some ideas to nudge you into the right direction. Women in their stupidity then allowed it, but the women cannot take all the blame for this one. We cannot blame women for allowing it though because realistically men, women are nurturers. Men will take advantage of this though. How can a single woman raising a man teach him the qualities of men; we are losing. We cannot ladies. Stop thinking just because you have superwoman tendencies you can teach a boy to be a man no matter how strong you are. Fellows we have to start building our family so we can have a new breed of men in the world who want to pursue educations, dreams, and financial goals early in life. We cannot constitute that it is okay to wait until your late 50's to get married to someone half your age and probably going to divorce in less than two years. Men, there are many women, good, classy, freaky, giving, hateful, whatever you like out there for you.

This is a plea from a woman to a man; we need more of the general population of men to want to have health relationships because we are killing our humanity. Think about this, if you are a man who goes to the club or stripe club to meet a woman keep in mind eventually you are going the figure the same ole everyday out will not change. Women understand this very well; when you're ready to change, on your own terms, you will. Women, we have to allow a man to figure himself out. We have to stop trying to think we can tell him

what he needs to change. Some men are so

far from changing, you have to tell yourself

"if he is the one for you" if not stop and

move on because guess what when you get

on his last nerve trying to make him change,

he is going to drop you like a bad habit and

move on. Then his problem thereafter he

will hate woman trying to change him and

now he goes and dogs out more women just

as much. This is a never ending cycle which

really needs to be broken. For example, we

have to support black love and rebuild

family foundation for black relationships.

We are now at an age where black men and

women are more financially stable, educated, and own their own business before the age of thirty but we cannot seem to get it right as a couple or mates.

Men this is a plea, please stop not being considerate. We will take advice from you rather if it's needed or not. Women will listen to your triumphant and tragedies even if she is a part of it or not. Women hear your life stories over and over and act as if it's her first time hearing it every time. Soon as she discuss aspirations, experiences, or her own knowledge it considered complaining. Do not minimize her knowledge because we all have walked different paths in this life.

And if you can get it off your chest she should be able to get it off of hers.

Men this is plea to begin or start back looking at our women as beautiful Queens. Plea to black men please stop allowing the media and magazines tell you only white or other race of women are more beautiful than the black woman who was created for you. Think about this, men, Asian marry their own, Italians marry their own, and Latino's marry their own. What is the problem? Do not be blinded. I understand love is love no matter the race but my plea is to begin to understand we are dying out in the fashion of black love.

Chapter 9

Bottom feeding women

Yes, the bottom feeders. This is any woman who does not respect herself first and she does not respect the next woman. She will not care about her fellow woman in any regards. Men love to see you coming because they can treat you like dirt, put you in the most griming situations, having any type of pleasures with you, and tell you anything. The sadness is the bottom feeder will in turn blame her fellow woman the faults she carriers. For example, "she slipping, if her man wants to get with me I am going to let him" like she is the one with the penis or predatory instincts. Plainly said you are naive. This type of woman can be dangerous to both men and women. The reason I say this is she has no value not only concerning of herself but her life. Men, you might think it is fun and cool to have relations with these type of women but it's not. They do not care who they have sex with to for fill whatever void they are trying to fill. She's dangerous because she will tell both the man and the woman of her involvement in her twisted triangle that she's not going anywhere. Men if you find yourself in a situation where you're trying to break it off with this type of chic, I mean in the worse way as possible, and she tells you she not going anyway, that a serious statement? Women, have you ever been caught up in a triangle with a chic like this and you confront her on the phone and she directly tells you "Bitch I'm not going nowhere, I am still going be fucking him, I am always going to be waiting in the cut for him, girl he can't leave me alone, I'm his first love, or I can't wait until he gets over your ass?" If you've been told anything remotely close to this, please be mindful this type of chic will do anything. This includes harm you or give you HIV/AIDS. Men this is a red flag for you as well, to think it is cute to go back and forth with a person who mental state is at this level. Snapped is a documentary show of real cases. Think about that one. Women run for the hills, if you find yourself in a triangle like this. Murder rates of spouses and partner triangles base on adultery and infidelity has tripled in the last three years. We have to get since of self, back. No need for me to continue to address bottom feeders because if you are one and reading this you are already mad as hell and cursing this book out. Usually these are the parties who love the continuous drama of the whole fiasco.

For kicks and giggles I am more or less

speaking to a brick wall. Bottom-line this is

considered deranged mentally. Pay attention

ladies if a man likes to continuously to have

such drama around him that is no good for

you if you want your life.

Chapter 10

Compelled

It is very important each of us love ourselves independently of someone else loving you. We have to get out of the bitter, mean party. Our essence of being of women has the stigma of holding a grudge, angry all the time. Stop it, the reflection of your being and your surrounding can impact you. Clean your house, stop holding on to what Craig 'em did to you years ago and stop gossiping about your personal business or problems. Give yourself the opportunity to keep an open mind, not a stupid mind. You cannot be upset that you met the wrong guy or have the wrong baby daddy. It's life. Pray and learn to let it go. No person wants to be around bitter people, reminding you how you remind them of their bitter past. Or better yet those people who put you in a generalized category of all men or all women. EACH PERSON has their own DNA and fingerprint, so why not let the one person who broke your heart take on that responsibility not the rest of those you met after the fact. Have you ever thought to yourself or wondered why you look at good functioning couples and get upset or depress. In some cases envy kicks in. Those two individuals you see that have healthy functional relationship, probably was that same person you past up on years ago. It might not be that exact person but it could have been the same person with those manners, charisma, humorous, driven heart, and passion you are looking for now. You just did not recognize it and you still do not know how to recognize it. Have you ever wondered why people who keep their lives private have mastered the art of telling you about themselves? Think about it they do it in way where you think you know a lot about them. And the feeling of knowing or thinking you know a lot about them satisfies you. Women you are so gullible to this. Understand the destruction is to make you feel secure enough to allow whatever comes next to happen. So by the time you realize it, puff in the wind. Whatever "puff in the wind" means to you put it here. Take ownership, your fault. Every relationship needs a compelling future; understand each other at the start. Men let's work on this; by stop leaving a trail of broken hearts it is bound to catch up with you and kill you. Women let's work on this; by stop allowing stupidity in and greeting it with your vagina, it is by far bound to destroy you. People show their character, feelings, and imagery

of themselves unconsciously by their

behavior. Understand and relate to what you

attract in partnership, relationship, and

companionships. Ask yourself do I attract

the same type of person? Then ask yourself

why? It could be that you hang out in the

same areas all the time. It could be you hang

out with the same setting of people all the

time. It could be that this is where you are

best comfortable because no one wants to go

outside their "ouch zone". This is any facet

of your life where you find it difficult to

create new beginnings or new ventures. The

first steps are always the hardest but

Who Do I Have to BE?

remember it can always lead to different
results.

ABOUT THE AUTHOR

Gracy Henderson is a very talented visionary who has proven to be a well-received inspiration of knowing self-worth, advocate of changing your mindset, and awarding contributions and services to others. She is well versed in accounting, criminal justice specializing in forensics, and inspiring philanthropist for women.

www.ingramcontent.com/pod-product-compliance
Lightning Source LLC
LaVergne TN
LVHW011913080426
835508LV00007BA/505